STARK ARTHOLOGY

STARK COUNTY ART • STARK COUNTY ARTISTS

Clare Murray Adams
Diann Adams
Sandy Adams
Kevin Anderson
Jeremy Aronhalt
Laura Barry
Tim Belden
Diane Belfiglio
Vicki Boatright a.k.a. "BZTAT"
Craig "Uncle Dreg" Booth
Brandon Bowman
John M. Branham
Brittney Breckenridge
Renie Britenbucher
Patrick G. Buckohr
Jerry Adam Burris
Martin A. Chapman
Michele Cimprich
Joseph Carl Close
Carol R. DeGrange
Frank Dale
Lynn Digby
George DiSabato
Marti Jones Dixon
Steve Ehret
Donna Fuchs
Carolyn Jacob
Robert Joliet
Laura Kolinski-Schultz
Judi Krew
Bili Kribbs
David Kuntzman
Ted Lawson
Jeff Lowe
Billy Ludwig
Joanne Mariol
Brett Marriner
Megan Mars
Tiffany Marsh
Joe Martino
Nancy Stewart Matin
Bob Maurer
Sharon Frank Mazgaj
David McDowell
Stephen McNulty
Thom Metz
Wanda Montgomery
Erin T. Mulligan
Su Nimon
Scot Phillips
Tina Puckett
Mieze Riedel
Pat Ripple
Priscilla Roggenkamp
William Shearrow
Sarah Winther Shumaker
Hurshel Smith
Brittany Steigert
Judith Sterling
John Strauss
Christopher J. Triner
Angelina Verginis
Fredlee Votaw
Michele Waalkes
Michael Weiss
Keith Wilson
Shawn Wood
Isabel Zaldivar
Derek Zimmerman

Edited by Jessica Bennett

Foreword by David C. Kaminski
Photography by Michael Barath,
Tim Belden & Thom Metz

indigo
ink
PRESS

STARK ARTHOLOGY
STARK COUNTY ART • STARK COUNTY ARTISTS

Library of Congress Control Number: 2010932350

ISBN: 978-0-9828330-0-1

Printed and bound in the United States of America by
The Covington Group, Kansas City, Missouri

10 9 8 7 6 5 4 3 2 1

Indigo Ink Press, Inc.
150 35th Street NW
Canton, Ohio 44709
www.IndigoInkPress.org

CONTENTS

FOREWORD

"Mini Bittner" is the title of the watercolor painting on the cover of this book. It is the work of Ted Lawson of Canton, Ohio, and it depicts the famous Taggart's ice cream parlor on Fulton Road NW in Canton, home of the equally famous Bittner Special sundae. Ted and 68 fellow artists have been chosen to show their work in "Stark ARThology," the first title published by the nonprofit Indigo Ink Press of Canton, Ohio. You may ask, Where did Ted come from? Where did Indigo Ink come from?

Until his retirement in April 2010, Ted was an engineer at Marathon Petroleum in Canton, schooled in mechanical engineering and economics. So, how did this mechanical engineer become a watercolor artist? The better question, Lawson thinks, is how did an artist become a mechanical engineer? "I always liked drawing, knew I could draw, but had to make a living." He said that he decided to study watercolor painting about 15 years ago and trained under Bette Elliott, whom he describes as "the grandmother of watercolor in Stark County." Elliott "was my mentor that guided me onto my own path, a very freeing experience." Lawson's interpretive images begin with photographs of his subject. You would not have seen him with an easel in front of Taggart's, creating the painting that became this book's cover.

There are 68 other artists in this book with stories to tell. Meet one. Ask one why and how. Enjoy these photos of their work. Appreciate Stark County as the home of so many creative people. And keep an eye out for what Indigo Ink Press does next.

In "Stark ARThology," Indigo Ink has two goals: to showcase visual arts in this community, and to establish the press as an artistic presence of its own. In this community of visual art, how does a publishing house make an impression? The literary arts require quiet, patience, time, and perhaps a cozy chair in your living room. None of those ingredients are much like a walk through Canton's gallery district during a First Friday festival.

Indigo Ink's strategy: In the initial months of existence for the publishing house, earn support from ArtsinStark, the County Arts Council. Do so by proposing to publish a book about the visual arts. Make a success of publishing and selling it. In the process, introduce people to Indigo Ink Press, a Canton-based publishing house. Then hit them with a novel or a book of poetry and see what happens. That's the plan that Indigo Ink founder Jessica Bennett has in mind.

An artist and his art. A publisher and her dream. It's what got you this far.

Dive in. Enjoy.

DAVID C. KAMINSKI

THE PHOTOGRAPHERS

Michael Barath is a photographer and educator from Canton. He teaches at Stark State College where he has assisted in the development of their Digital Photography Program. His favorite subjects are his three golden retrievers and two grandchildren, Hannah and Ayden, all five of whom shed terribly.

More info: www.JustUsTwo.com

Tim Belden is an entrepreneur whose most recent project is the Joseph Saxton Gallery of Photography, located in the center of the city block that he is redeveloping in downtown Canton's Arts District. He studied creative writing and art history at Bowling Green and Cornell Universities.

More info: www.JosephSaxton.com

Thom Metz is originally from the Canton South area. He was a professional photographer and lab technician at 16, and it was his passion until his early 20s, when a career change consumed him and other priorities took over. He has since returned to the creative world of photography.

More info: www.Myspace.com/metzcraft

INTRODUCTION

This book has taught me an important truth - to see the art is to know the artist.

It's true. Thumb through these pages for even a few moments and you'll see in short order that each artist describes their essence far more acutely through their work than through their words. Every morsel is in there - the concessions and the contradictions, the hopes and fears, the ecstasy and outrage, the obsession and indifference. It's all there, waiting to be understood.

> *"Use what language you will, you can never say anything but what you are."*
>
> RALPH WALDO EMERSON

The words they use are most often simple trappings - means to an end that they think you, the reader, expect to have provided. And you do, don't you? But it's the work that is the unexpected, the honest. The work comes from the gut. The words are a well done fake, a counterfeit; the art is the genuine article.

I can try to tell you in my words what I hope you will experience in these pages, but it would be in vain.

Words are not the currency of character here - the language of the day is not in the text that accompanies each work. The essence of these works, and thus, the constitution of these artists, cannot be discerned by the language with which you are accustomed. Once you have had the experience for yourself - once you have let yourself be swallowed up by the exhibit bound on these pages, you'll have to agree.

This book was born out of a need to support the artists in our community. On the whole, we do a good job of supporting "the arts" - that abstract, intangible entity that finds itself so often paired with "culture." Where we struggle is in supporting the individual artists. We support the whole, but not the part. This book is for the part, for the microcosm, for the singular soul - not for the system.

That's what we hope to accomplish through Indigo Ink, too. To reveal the distinct essence of each of our storytellers or artists through their own works. To abandon convention, to obliterate the old adage that a whole is the sum of its parts.

Whole be damned, we want to put the parts on parade.

Please enjoy this, our first parade.

And I think you'll see that this book doesn't need a dedication page.

It has 69 of them.

JESSICA BENNETT

EVIDENCE OF IDENTITY NO. 3
MIXED MEDIA ASSEMBLAGE,
20" x 20", © 2009

CLARE MURRAY ADAMS

My work explores themes of memory that are both personal and collective. It is interesting to reflect on an experience and see it unfold itself in the guise of memory. Through the processes of experiencing, storing and remembering, I want to get below the surface and express that which may be tentative and somewhat elusive. Aspects of memory are undeniably linked to identity. They are vessels that carry emotion and connect us to each other. My work is meant to reveal, through its use of fabric, collage and encaustic paint, references to the human condition, which can be sometimes quite personal and at other times more universal, but almost always a revelation.

Clare Murray Adams is a professor of art and former chair of the Visual Art Department at Malone University. She received a BFA from Kent State University and an MFA from Vermont College. Over the past 25 years, her fiber and mixed media work has been exhibited and honored regionally and nationally. During the past two years she has had six solo exhibits in Ohio, Indiana, New York, South Carolina and California.

CONTACT: www.ClareMurrayAdams.com

FUMED IN THE FIRE URN
PORCELAIN, 7" x 6", © 2010

DIANN ADAMS

I never liked to play in the mud as a child, but I've always enjoyed function, form and color. As an adult, I play in the mud all the time. I am amazed at how mud transforms itself with just a little pushing and pulling. I create functional and non-functional work. My goal is to brighten lives with a little piece of clay that transcends all barriers and is what it is. I am crazed about Raku and in awe of the pitfiring process. These processes are so unpredictable, yet they produce wonderful colors on pottery pieces... that is assuming the pottery survives the thermal shock of the process!

Diann Adams is a lifelong fine artist. In 1967, she was awarded the Martha Holden Jennings Award for students in fine arts and received a scholarship to Chautaugua Institute, where she studied painting. She also attended Wilmington College, majoring in fine art. She has an associate's degree in applied sciences from Kent State University at Ashtabula. She is the vice president of the Canton Ceramic Artist Guild in Canton, Ohio. She has studied ceramics and pottery at the Canton Museum of Art under Laura Kolinski-Schultz and William Shearrow. She was named "Hearted Artist" by Heart Stark Art, and has a permanent gallery at their website (HeartStarkArt.org), as well as online galleries at Laguna Clay and the Potters' Council.

CONTACT: www.EarthToArtCeramics.etsy.com

MONTANA MORNING
PHOTOGRAPHY, © 2009

SANDY ADAMS

Nature photography has been a love of mine for many years. The fulfillment is in the whole process. The quiet awareness of being in nature, the challenge of finding and capturing the beauty of natural compositions and the excitement and joy of viewing and sharing them.

My goal is to artistically transfer the emotion and beauty I see and feel when I take the photograph to the eye of the viewer to enjoy over and over again.

Sandy Adams has been an Ohio nature photographer for over 20 years, taking photographs in many of the surrounding parks, gardens and bogs of Stark County. She's been a member of The Wilderness Center Photography Club and serves as vice president. She has participated in art shows at the Canton Museum of Art. Awards for her nature photography include the Wilderness Center Foto Fest, CJCC Annual Northeast Ohio Photography Show, Wildlife Garden, Ohio Environmental Council, and various other local and nature-related contests. One of her award-winning photographs was recently published on the cover of the Ohio Environmental Council Newsletter.

CONTACT: SandyAdams@sssnet.com

KEVIN ANDERSON

My vision is to create original, three-dimensional products that intimately or dramatically affect people. I strive for work that is creative, smart and/or provocative. I design functional art, mixing many diverse media into one unique product. All my pieces are original and hand built from raw materials by me. I am compulsive about the fit and finish, which is punctuated by my obsession with mathematics, geometry, pattern and texture. My work is often highlighted by my love of satire and parody.

Kevin Anderson attended the Cleveland Institute of Art, and began his work as a creative designer for General Motors. After five years in metro Detroit, he set up his own design studio. His niche is in professionally fabricating creative furnishings and environments, with expertise in building furniture, molding and casting (plaster, concrete, resins and fiberglass), prototyping, product design, industrial design, model-building and mixed media sculpture. He owns and operates Anderson Creative Studio in downtown Canton, Ohio.

CONTACT: www.AndersonKevin.com

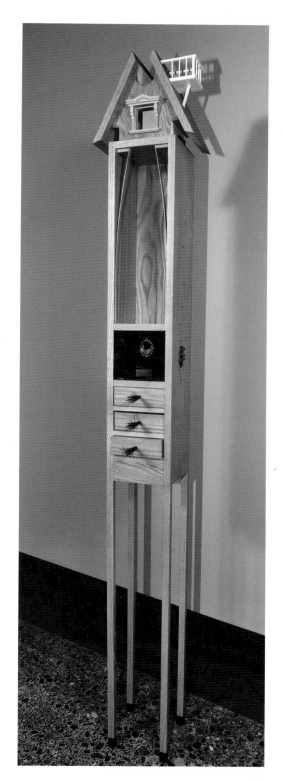

HOUSE ARREST
OAK, MAHOGANY AND POPLAR, ACRYLIC AND ENAMEL PAINT,
11" x 79" x 10", © 2010

JEREMY ARONHALT

I've been shooting photos since 1994. I started in high school, then just kept on going. About five years ago, I decided that this is how I want to make my living. Through hundreds of books and magazines, thousands of hours and dollars, I'm almost there.

My fiance and I are going full-time with A Studio Photography, our wedding, senior and family portrait business. I shoot art photography through Brown Bike Photography, my personal photography brand. I capture bands, BMX and motor-cycle shots, among other projects. Brown Bike Photography is named for a brown S&M dirt bike I bought when I was living in Oakland, Calif. I rode that bike for seven years and loved it! I met so many cool people when I traveled that year and that bike represented a great time in my life. I still have the bike, and while I ride a green one now, I'm not changing the name!

Jeremy Aronhalt is a photographer based in Canton, Ohio. He runs A Studio Photography with his wife.

CONTACT: www.BrownBikePhotography.com/blog

LAURA BARRY

In painting, I struggle to understand the relationship between the natural environment and the synthetic, manmade world we have created for ourselves. My paintings incorporate elements from both worlds in an effort to find a balance between the two. Ultimately, through this juxtaposition of imagery, I hope to open up a dialogue on humanity's relationship to nature.

Laura Barry was born in Akron, Ohio, and raised in North Canton, Ohio. In 2009, she graduated with a bachelor's of fine art from Miami University in Oxford, Ohio, with a concentration in painting and ceramics. Barry's approach to art is influenced by her interest in environmental science and the rise of technology in our modern world. These influences are incorporated into her materials. Barry has recently switched to using only non-toxic acrylic paint, as well as making her own paint from dirt and acrylic medium. She has traveled to Norway, Greece, England and France to immerse herself in art and culture. She currently lives and works in Northeast Ohio.

CONTACT: www.LauraBarry.carbonmade.com

LAST ONE STANDING
ACRYLIC ON UNPRIMED CANVAS, 3' x 6', © 2009

TIM BELDEN

I am mainly interested in history, mythology and aesthetics. An avid collector of anything that appeals to a crow, I assemble artifacts in ways that yield distinct interpretations.

As an English major, I'm also interested in rhetoric, and its relationship with a photographic image. Photography can employ figurative modes of expression, like poetry.

Tim Belden started in photography as a teenager, using his sister's basement darkroom. He partnered in his first art gallery in 1975-76, and graduated from Bowling Green State University with a major in creative writing and minor in art history. His graduate degree was in creative writing from Cornell in 1988.

He opened the Joseph Saxton Gallery of Photography in 2009.

CONTACT: www.JosephSaxton.com

ROTHKO'S WINE
PHOTOGRAPHY, © 2010

DIANE BELFIGLIO

My acrylic on canvas paintings have always prominently featured closely-cropped, sunlit architectural forms. Although realistic in their presentation, I rely heavily on their underlying abstract qualities to give the already imposing images an even greater sense of power. Shadows, ethereal by nature, take on a rigid, structural aspect in my compositions. Colors range from brilliant to subtle in an effort to reproduce the strong sense of sunlight streaming through each piece.

Although these images are visually powerful, the delicate details in the architecture - and often in the surrounding vegetation - are also prominently featured in my work. The resultant blend produces a heightened, stylized reality. I work to transform the mundane into the extraordinary, so that we see beauty in images that generally go unnoticed by most of us on a daily basis.

Diane Belfiglio earned her BFA in drawing, painting, and graphics from The Ohio State University, and her MFA in painting from Syracuse University. She has exhibited in well over 150 group and solo shows regionally, nationally and internationally. Belfiglio's works are included in 12 corporate art collections and numerous private collections, including the collection of singer Patti LaBelle. In addition, her work is now in the permanent collections of the It-chiku Kubota Art Museum in Tokyo, Japan, and The Butler Institute of American Art in Youngstown, Ohio. She has taught part-time at several universities and is currently an adjunct professor at Walsh University in North Canton, Ohio, where she also resides.

CONTACT: www.Belfiglio.com

ASCENT WITH GERANIUMS
ACRYLIC, 33" x 49", © 1997

VICKI BOATRIGHT

A.K.A. BZTAT

A lot of art serves to provoke, intimidate, shock, titillate and sometimes, even violate. It all has its place, but there is also a place for less disturbing art. There is some value to this statement by Henri Matisse: "What I dream of is an art of balance, of purity and serenity devoid of troubling or depressing subject matter - a soothing, calming influence on the mind, rather like a good armchair, which provides relaxation from physical fatigue."

I like the fact that my work often brings a sense of joy to people, lifting their emotions through color, texture and context. I do, however, have artwork that is more expressive and challenging. Even so, I seek balance and hope in each work of art. That is the nature of my soul and what is in me to create.

Vicki Boatright known as "BZTAT" (pronounced bee-zee-tat), specializes in whimsical drawings, paintings and digital images of cats, dogs and other companion animals. She has completed a number of public and private art commissions along with community art, public art, murals and social service projects. She holds a BFA and MFA in the visual arts and a master's degree in counseling from Marshall University in Huntington, W.Va. Boatright is an active writer and is well known in the global blogosphere.

CONTACT: www.BZTAT.com

CRAIG "UNCLE DREG" BOOTH

When my brother, Brennis Booth, and his partner, Todd Walburn, opened up 2nd April Galerie, I knew I wanted to be a part of it. So I found an old Minolta 35mm camera in my dad's closet. After snapping about 20 rolls of film, I figured out how to take a picture. Since, I've started experimenting with all kinds of different techniques. I like to call it "digital art photography." It's a medium that combines the traditional elements of photography with the ever-evolving technology of digital cameras, computers and graphic design. That's why I like it. It keeps changing. What may be true in the medium this year, may be totally different next year. There's a saying that "every picture tells a story." That's what I like to do with my pictures. Sometimes those stories are good and sometimes they're bad. I like to tell both sides of the story. I like to twist perceptions of things people see every day. I also think some pictures just look cool up on the wall.

Craig "Uncle Dreg" Booth was born and raised in Canton, Ohio. He is a self-taught artist who started taking pictures in 2000. In 2008, he opened his own studio, The Dreg Spot, inside 2nd April Galerie in downtown Canton. He also works for the City of Canton Water Department.

CONTACT: UncleDreg.Tripod.com

BRANDON BOWMAN

My life has been filled with adventure, experience and excitement. From a very young age, art has been a major part of my life. It has been nurtured and constantly encouraged in me. When I say young, I do mean *young* - from the time that I could hold a pencil I have been creating and developing the necessary skills to create works of art (special thanks to my father for this). Many artists attempt to master one medium or one discipline of the many available forms of visual art, but that has never been and will never be enough for me. I believe that if it can be done by someone else, then I can do it also.

I appreciate and enjoy almost any and all art. I am not fond of any self-proclaimed "artist" who justifies their work or their unearned title by using the bullshit statement "there are no rules," or "rules are meant to be broken." You cannot break the rules of traditional art, without first leaning them.

Brandon Bowman is a graduate of Kent State University with two bachelor's degrees in fine and professional arts and in art education. He currently teaches art at GlenOak High School in Canton, Ohio.

CONTACT: www.Artova.com

18

JOHN M. BRANHAM

I consider what I do digital illustration, or more specifically, photo manipulation with some mixed media, drawing and painting thrown in the mix.

John M. Branham graduated from The University of Akron with a bachelor's degree in fine arts and graphic design. He works full-time and freelances as a designer and artist in digital art/mixed media.

CONTACT: zombietronart@gmail.com

SELF-PORTRAIT
DIGITAL, © 2009

BRITTNEY BRECKENRIDGE

My practice is driven by the connection between art and ecology. Fragility, time, nature, and humanity's loss of connection with the Earth are a part of my work. I try to show in my work that humanity needs to make an impression that transcends time. Our presence on this earth is profound, and so is our desire to archive and display the objects that define our humanity. The representation of our culture and creativity, and how we relate to nature, are sure to continue to be the focus of my future work.

Brittney Breckenridge is a graduate of the Maryland Institute College of Art in Baltimore, Md,, where she focused on printmaking and mixed media. Currently, she has returned to Ohio to obtain her master's in arts administration. She has been awarded numerous scholarships and awards, including the Ohio Distinguished Artist Award, the MICA Trustee Scholarship and the Ohio Governor's Art Award.

CONTACT: www.BrittneyBreckenridge.com

BORN READY
SCREENPRINT, 12" x 28", © 2008

RENIE BRITENBUCHER

I love to paint and I love to bring a sense of joy to the viewer of my work. That's the goal for me. I focus on joyful childhood memories and other positive thoughts and feelings as I paint.

I've been doing an ongoing series called "Peace on Earth" and figure it's my little contribution to peace for the world we live in.

Renie Britenbucher is an artist from Canton, Ohio. She has been painting for 30 years and her work can be seen throughout the United States, Canada, Australia, Asia and Europe. Her work portrays a whimsical joy and many times, humor. She is known for her Diva series, which feature above average-sized women, many times on the beach or in precarious situations. She is also known for her Jazz and Blues themed work and her whimsical folk art. Britenbucher is honored to be a winner in the annual Artists' Choice Awards (ACA), voted for by fellow artists on eBay, for the last several years. She has recently signed on to be represented by Cruise Creative, an art licensing agency, and hopes to see her work on some products in the near future.

CONTACT: www.RenieBritenbucher.com

PEACE ON EARTH
ACRYLIC, 20" x 16", © 2010

RHINO
RECYCLED STEEL & TIRES
10' x 5' x 7', © 2009

PATRICK G. BUCKOHR

Every day I work harder at being a better artist. It's all I've ever wanted to do since that first discovery of art at age six. It's that sensation of discovery, of giving life to something, telling a story or sometimes just watching it happen at the hands of my peers. It's telling. It's an energy that every really, really good artist I've ever met knows about, like some kind of secret handshake. More than any of that, it is work and we can see those scars in each other. There is no bohemian fantasy. It's work - just dirty, rarely glamorous and sometimes plain dangerous work. At least that's from where the good art comes.

Patrick G. Buckohr expands his odd imagination into art, exploring beyond traditional media to express his unique way of looking at our world. He creates more for his own curiosity than acclaim or approval - more than anything he wants to make art that tells stories. Following a graphic design education at The University of Akron, he had a 15-year career in printing and publishing, before following his sideline passions into a career as a painter and sculptor. Buckohr has been part of many regional shows, exhibits and festivals. He has created many public murals and sculptures, including critters from reclaimed steel, and of course, a rhino made from recycled tires.

CONTACT: www.Facebook.com/buckohr

JERRY ADAM BURRIS

My methodology is very simple when it comes to producing images. Cause and effect play a major role in my thought process. What would my plate look like if I took it outside and threw it around on the sidewalk? I wonder what this photo would look like if I took off my shirt, scanned it, and color burned it over top? Can I destroy my charcoal drawing with an eraser and still have it hold meaning to the viewer?

Most of these things that go through my head deal with destruction and abuse of the media. Destruction can be done physically when dealing with printmaking because of the physical nature of working with something tangible like a zinc plate. Digital abuse is far more complex. I prefer incorporating different elements into an image that don't always go along with the subject. Handwritten notes, sketches, and doodles can create elaborate textures that can add or subtract a lot from an image. All of these processes are what I call forced mistakes. These accidents are what cause me to explore different directions. They don't always work but that is what is truly great about process, it is figuring out which mistakes to keep.

Jerry Adam Burris graduated from Louisville High School in 2003 and from Ohio Wesleyan University with a bachelor's of fine arts in 2007. He is currently working on a master's of visual arts curriculum and instruction at The University of Akron. Burris works as a freelance graphic designer, videographer and assistant football coach at Louisville High School.

CONTACT: www.coroflot.com/burris

SETTING FOOT IN THE DOORWAY OF INCOMPLETION: TOMORROW AS AN AFTERTHOUGHT
DIGITAL DESIGN, © 2008

MARTIN A. CHAPMAN

When I began turning wood about six years ago, little did I suspect that it would become a time-consuming passion. I started turning because I have access to lots of green hardwood on our 60-acre farm in southeastern Stark County and I had the rudiments of the necessary tools to make irregular shaped wood take on some sort of regular and maybe planned shape.

It doesn't always work out quite the way I plan or envision, but whatever the project, the wood always finds its own voice. Sometimes it screams "how can you do this to me?" and other times it coos "ooh, that feels good," but as turners have found for over three thousand years, the wood never lies. It is what it is. Once it was firewood; now it's a work of art. Perhaps someday it'll be firewood again.

Martin A. Chapman is a retired prosecutor, attorney, former teacher and broadcast journalist who took his first woodturning class in 2003. He has a wood shop on his farm near Minerva, Ohio, and his turned objects are exhibited in several galleries in Northeast Ohio. He regularly demonstrates turning on his mini-lathe in schools and for civic groups and clubs. He is a member of the American Association of Woodturners, the Ohio Arts and Crafts Guild and a local turning club.

CONTACT: lawmart@aol.com

MICHELE CIMPRICH

I have been drawn to forgotten, weathered and abandoned places and objects as long as I can remember. Knowing that someone once lived, loved and persevered in these homes, their gardens, and other structures evokes a reverence in me. Botanical subjects have become a favorite of mine to shoot as well. I am obsessed with their structure and forms, textures and growth patterns over time.

I have a deep appreciation for the fragile existence of all things - their growth, death and decay with the passage of time. By capturing such on film, I honor and reveal a grandness, forcing the viewer to observe anew.

Michele Cimprich is a graduate of the University of Notre Dame with a bachelor's degree in graphic design and photography. She has been exhibiting and selling her work for the last 15 years at juried fine art shows and select galleries all over the Midwest. She has been honored to receive numerous awards for her work. She and her husband are horticulturists and work together running a retail garden center in Peninsula, Ohio.

CONTACT: wanderingpaths@earthlink.net

INVITATION...
PHOTOGRAPHY, © 2002

BURDEN
STEEL AND FOUND METAL, 7' x 2.5' x 3', © 2008

JOSEPH CARL CLOSE

Mythology is a subject that is as mysterious as it is informative to me. I love to tweak existing stories and build a framework around characters both real and imagined, bringing them to life in an epic that I have been chasing for some time now. I take what is available in my physical reality - oil, glass, steel and discarded furniture, and deconstruct them into a fantasy world of heroes and villains, creating a matrix of characters that deal with the psychological nature of myself and the world around me.

Mostly self taught, **Joseph Carl Close** has come across many individuals with diverse skill sets, such as hand blown glass, steel fabrication, carpentry and oil painting, allowing him to develop these skills and craft a found object world that is ever-evolving. Born in Columbus, Ohio, Close met fellow artist and craftsman KC Carter. The glass blower took Close on as an assistant in 2001 to help relocate and build a hot shop from the ground up. Close has been working in and around Canton, Ohio, ever since. With commissioned work including a 90 ft. long steel mural, to scrap metal bonsai trees, this Ohio artist has carved a living by being as diverse as possible. Oil painting is the true passion for Close, allowing him to develop a mythological framework to tell stories.

CONTACT: josephcloseart@yahoo.com

CAROL R. DeGRANGE

When I began working with photography, I started to see the world in a completely different way, both the microcosm and the macrocosm.

Carol R. DeGrange is a retired teacher who became interested in photography during her time teaching in China. She taught British and American literature and culture at Don Bei Dian Li Xue Yuan, an electrical engineering institute in Manchuria, and Sun-Yat-Sen University in Guangzhou, China. She has also taught Oriental art, English and American literature at the University of Mount Union in Alliance, and Walsh University in North Canton. DeGrange has written a mystery novel, *The Ming Legacy*, set in China, and she is currently working on her second novel.

CONTACT: degrangec@neo.rr.com

CHINESE SHOES DRYING IN WINDOW
PHOTOGRAPHY, © 1989

FRANK DALE

When I was a young boy, I remember seeing a beautiful oil painting in a doctor's waiting room. A landscape with a house and a windmill. My mother said it had been done by a German or Dutch painter. The surface had a deep gloss, and the color values went from deep transparent umbers to brilliant yellow-orange sunlight. I knew instantly that I wanted to learn how to make paint look deep and brilliant like that. But growing up in the Great Depression, there was never any money for luxuries, and I was a senior in high school before I got my first paint set. I was very disappointed, however, when my first painting dried and the colors turned dull and lifeless. They did not have the depth, the transparent glow I had seen in that first painting. One Sunday in Golden Gate Park, I saw an old man painting a landscape that had the shiny surface and glowing colors I was looking for. I rushed up to him, wild with excitement, and asked what he used for his medium. He turned to me and said in the most unfriendly voice, "I spent a lifetime figuring it out. Do you think I'm just going to give it away?"

I swore to myself that if I ever figured it out, I would share my discoveries with anyone who wanted to know. The search to discover the secrets of those Old Master paintings remained fruitless until many years later. Using a technique based on the Flemish painters and old recipes using natural tree resins, my paintings began to acquire the transparent glow that I had been seeking, and my work began to win awards. Soon people were asking to take lessons. I have now taught privately over 30 students how to paint. My first student, who started when she was sixteen, has since graduated from college and teaches art in a private school in North Carolina. I continue to share my knowledge with anyone who asks, from adolescents to retirees. Because I do not tell students what to paint, only how, each student's work displays a very wide variety of subject matter.

Frank Dale has been drawing pictures since before he was in grade school. He did his first oil painting at the age of 18. He studied art in Northern California where he grew up, attending The California School of Fine Arts in San Francisco and San Francisco State Teacher's College in the late fifties and early sixties. Since retiring from business in 1999, Dale has been able to devote all of his time to drawing, painting and teaching the Flemish technique to his many students. He was an active Signature Member of the Akron Society of Artists and served three terms on the Board of Directors. He served as the scholarship committee chairman for ASA until 2010. He was the visual arts director for the Stow Family Arts Festival, held in conjunction with Kent State's Aviation Day in September 2001. His oil paintings, as well as his students, have won many awards, ranging from honorable mention to Best of Show. Dale resides in Massillon, Ohio, where he teaches oil painting and paints oil portraits and other interesting things.

CONTACT: dulcipix@aol.com

LYNN DIGBY

I love the human form and face, and I find myself wanting to explore the tactile quality of surfaces, as well as the inherent grace of the person I paint. I have no interest in cynicism, preferring instead to look candidly at who the person is, how they present themselves, and communicate my empathy with that. My portraits do not attempt to glamorize my subjects, but rather they strive to reveal the authentic person that I see. Since I like people, this view tends to be empathetic rather than critical or jaundiced. I try to reveal a certain atmospheric density; a saturated stillness that is often missed in observation from life.

Lynn Digby considers herself a self-taught artist, despite having her bachelor's in art education. Her current work reflects more about where her interests lie now than it does her (mostly modernist) training in school. She taught art in the public schools for 25 years, and retired in 2008. Currently, she is a full-time painter, specializing in portraiture, her first love. She is thrilled to be involved in the Canton Arts District, a place where creativity runs rampant.

CONTACT: www.LynnDigby.artspan.com

THAT DAMNED WOMAN
OIL, 18" x 24", © 2008

GEORGE DiSABATO

All my work has been derived in some way from the landscape, from landscape painters or even from paintings I saw as landscapes. I have found similarities in everything from Chinese landscapes, Japanese prints, Persian miniatures, medieval Italian painting, Spanish influences, cubism and the New York School. I believe all of these styles to possess universal visual principles, and I hope to somehow continue in my own amalgam of those traditions through this Ohio form and color.

I have needed to work through nearly literal landscapes into the abstraction that keeps calling me. The joy is in the journey and the journey is, in Kandinsky's concept, spiritual not physical. I want this work to be related to the modernist revolution, not the post-modern counter-revolution; I want work that is visual, not verbal.

George DiSabato is professor emeritus of The University of Akron. He holds a bachelor's degree in painting from The Ohio State University and an MFA from the University of Louisville. He has studied and shown in Ohio, Kentucky, New York and Rhode Island.

CONTACT: george.disabato@yahoo.com

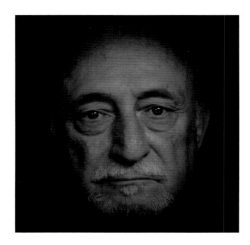

McCLUSKY PLACE
OIL, 22" x 30", © 2000

HILLARY
OIL, 12" x 16", © 2009

MARTI JONES DIXON

Who was it that said, "Writing about music is like dancing about architecture?" Martin Mull? Peter Buck? Elvis Costello? Frank Zappa? I can't remember where I read that quote, but it aptly illustrates my feelings toward writing about art. Simply put, art is a feeling. If you are someone who has difficulty expressing your feelings to other humans, you probably will have difficulty discussing art.

I paint because I have to. It keeps me alive and focused. I wake up thinking about it and I go to bed thinking about it. I think about what I want to achieve with each painting. I usually can't express these thoughts because they are intangible feelings. Abstract. Complicated. Indescribable. I do know that I want to show life in my paintings and that it's made up of complex variables: movement, weight, light. I want the viewer to feel the life. No need for discussion, really. Stare at it for as long as you want. And more importantly, you are free to feel whatever you want.

Marti Jones Dixon is now a full-time painter, after having a career as an A&M/RCA recording artist. She graduated from Kent State with a degree in art. Just after college, the music career fell into her lap, leaving her little time for painting. As her daughter grows older and requires less and less of her time, she spends most of her days in her downtown Canton Arts District studio.

CONTACT: www.MartiJonesDixon.com

GUILT
OIL, 24" x 18", © 2009

STEVE EHRET

Some days I enjoy making things bloody, gross, dark, angry, ugly and oozing with slime. Other days I feel like making my creatures look awkward, confused, sketchy and possibly a bit sweaty. Some are just looking for a bite to eat, others may have just figured out the meaning to their very lives! Some of them have a reason to be in the piece and others may just have stumbled down the wrong road and ended up where they wish they hadn't. Everything I do, everyone I talk to and mostly every trip I take is a major influence on my pieces. It's ever changing and I hope it stays that way.

Finding inspiration at dusk, **Steve Ehret** paints canvases filled with phantasmal creatures and landscapes. His obscure scenes and psyches bob between terror and hilarity, influenced by abstract realms of experience. His uninhibited characters roam old vacant buildings and decaying structures reminiscent of his hometown, exposing pleasures and misfortunes in the twilight. He contrasts harmony and separateness within his work, using acrylic, spray paint and ink. By adding oil paints and organic materials, he infuses depth into his multidimensional works. Starting to paint only several years ago, Ehret has quickly built his reputation by exhibiting his work in Cleveland, San Francisco and at the Massillon Art Museum.

CONTACT: www.Lbstrclws.com

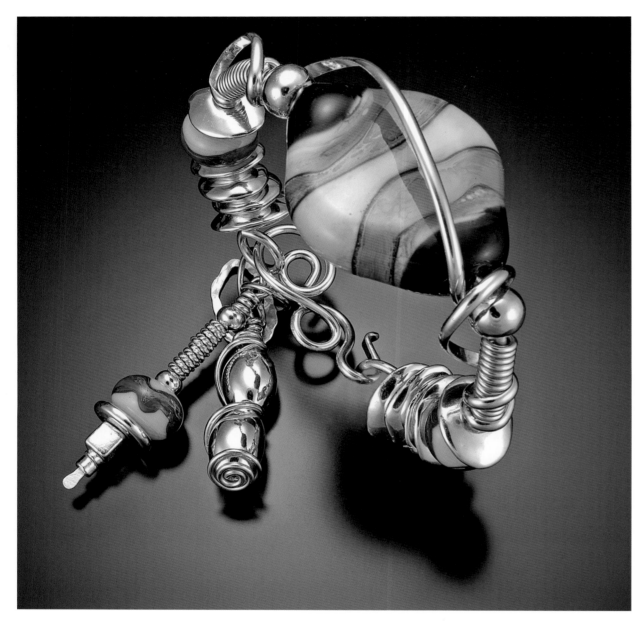

DONNA FUCHS

Each of my creations is unique, truly a one-of-a-kind piece. Since I work with natural materials from the earth and sea, they all have naturally-occurring variations. Each stone, piece of coral, metal and lampwork bead has its own individual beauty. That's part of what's wonderful about all things handmade! With this creative outlet, I am always discovering and learning something new.

Donna Fuchs grew up in a family of artists and was exposed to constant creativity: gospel music singers, painters, seamstresses and jewelry-makers. She studied art at the University of Tennessee in Nashville, and began her creative journey with painting. From there, she moved to contemporary quilt designing and quilt making, which led to years of designing specialty fabric items for many interior design firms. Her artistic evolution led her to jewelry, where she found her true passion. She designs bracelets, necklaces, pendants and earrings. Her work involves lampworking, wire wrapping, silversmithing, cold connecting and oxidizing. She is a certified instructor in the Precious Metal Clay (PMC) process, and teaches various art jewelry-making techniques at her home studio and other venues.

CONTACT: www.PenguinsNest.com

UNTITLED
HANDMADE GLASS BEADS WITH STERLING SILVER WIRE, © 2010
PHOTOGRAPH BY AZAD PHOTO, CORNVILLE, MAINE

CAROLYN JACOB

I have been exploring the beauty of our world through the camera's eye for over 50 years, and am constantly learning new techniques and seeing new ways to create images that speak to the viewer. I challenge myself to "see the picture in the picture," by selecting elements that may have been overlooked by traditional photography. I've found digital photography to offer a wide range of artistic opportunity - definitely appealing to my former graphic arts background. I am greatly encouraged to keep experimenting and expanding my horizons.

Carolyn Jacob is a New Jersey native, transplanted to Ohio during her college years at Wittenberg University. Jacob has worked as a graphic artist and previously owned Advertising Designs, a marketing resource for small businesses. She is currently employed by OBS Inc., a local specialty vehicle company, where she designs vehicle graphics and other promotional materials for trade shows and corporate marketing support. She also owns The ColorShoppe, Images for Interior Decor, which is based at 2nd April Galerie in downtown Canton. She has participated in various photography and art shows throughout Northeast Ohio and has received numerous awards.

CONTACT: www.CJPhotoHound.com

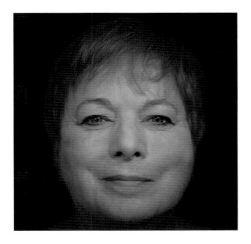

GHOST TRAIN
PHOTOGRAPHY, © 2009

ROBERT JOLIET

My vision is to create beautiful glass works of art in special settings, both interior and exterior. I achieve this through magnificent colors and glass textures. Personalizing each commission to the particular underlying specifications of landscape, lighting, flexibility and durability, I create one-of-a-kind art with glass and twisted metal.

Robert Joliet turned a fine arts degree, specializing in oil and watercolor, into a passion for stained glass. Joliet, along with is wife, Wendy, created Studio Arts & Glass over 28 years ago. Their commissions include custom-designed art glass windows, doors and skylights. In addition to designing leaded art glass, Joliet creates etched and carved glass designs. His designs can be found in restaurants, schools, hospitals, houses of worship and corporations, as well as private homes throughout North America. Studio Arts & Glass is located in North Canton, Ohio.

CONTACT: www.StudioArtsandGlass.com

LAURA KOLINSKI-SCHULTZ

My work reflects a strong interest in nature and in Chinese ceramic art, particularly the teaware of YiXing, China. The teaware is meant to be used! I enjoy the thought that I have a connection with the people who are using my work to brew tea, sip refreshing infusions and serve delicious meals.

Laura Kolinski-Schultz earned a bachelor's in art from The University of Mount Union and a bachelor's in art education from Kent State University. In addition, she has many hours of graduate study in art history and art education at KSU. Her specialty area is ceramic art. In 1996, 2001 and 2003, she studied with Taiwanese artists Yih Wen Kuo and Ah Leon at the Penland School of Craft in North Carolina. Currently, Kolinski-Schultz works with clay and teaches pottery in her home studio in Jackson Township and at the Canton Museum of Art. She is a member of the Canton Ceramic Artists Guild. Her new business, TerraKi Tea and Teaware, combines pottery, tea and Tai Chi. She presents Chinese tea ceremonies and lectures on tea, its cultivation, processing, history and benefits. Her hand-crafted, functional pottery is available at local art shows and by commission.

CONTACT: www.Terraki-Teaware.com

GREEN PUMPKIN TEAPOT
CERAMIC, 8.5" x 7.5", © 2010

JUDI KREW

I have been making art, selling art, donating art or teaching art for as long as I can remember. Art is in my blood and drives my soul. My talent is a gift from God. My personal imagery has included watercolor realism, xerography, photography, design and illustration, but my heart is in painting and drawing. My paintings are about women and our lives, the craziness of our society. They are intended to make the viewer laugh. My drawings are about capturing an expression or a moment, in color and with energy.

I have written many statements over my 30-year career and have come to realize that what I say about my work is not anywhere near as important as what my work can do to, and for, others, as well as what I can do for others as an artist. I have been blessed with the ability to make visual what others sometimes cannot see and for that I give thanks and I give back.

Judi Krew has participated in 118 regional and national juried exhibitions in 27 states, resulting in 30 awards for her work. She holds a bachelor's degree in fine art from The University of Akron (painting and drawing) and an MFA from Case Western Reserve University in art education. She is a charter member of the Canton Artists League, a member of the National Association of Women Artists and a MENSA member. When she isn't creating, she works as a substitute teacher for Jackson Local Schools and volunteers with a great many local organizations and charities.

CONTACT: www.JudiKrew.com

BILI KRIBBS

As children, we all absorbed pop culture: cartoons, the Muppets, video games, comic books and fantastical movies like Star Wars. So, my personal artwork reflects the constant, high-fructose, dancing fantasy that is fed to all of us by mass media as children. I am the product of TV-nurtured behavior. Marketing designed for children created my 30-second attention span and humor-laden thought process. Consumption of constant advertising jingles, cartoon fantasy violence and ridiculous humor eventually become inspirational. A fuel for creative outlet. Being an artist in this time allows for unlimited recourses of inspiration.

I have addictions to movies, television, cartoons, comic books, video games and toys. I am only an apprentice to what I am surrounded by. Creating is necessary for sanity in a time where we cannot ride in cars without music on, TVs are at the grocery store check-outs, and internet connections are on our portable communication devices. I have to get it out.

Someday I would like to produce more than I consume, but I am not entirely sure that will ever be possible.

Bili Kribbs is a graduate of the Art Institute of Pittsburgh with a degree in animation. His work has been displayed at several Massillon/Canton, Ohio, area art shows and galleries, including the annual Art is Alive event in Canton, and the Massillon Museum's Studio M shows. His animation credits include several shorts and two local television commercials. His work won Best in Show at the Stark County Artists Exhibit in 2008.

CONTACT: www.Bili.org

DESCARTES
ACRYLIC, 42" x 52", © 2008

DAVID KUNTZMAN

I have always been intrigued by the artworks labeled Op Art, Retinal Art, and "extreme abstraction," specifically the works of Vasarely, Stanczak and Riley. Not surprisingly, my earliest paintings were attempts to recreate the retinal experience with results of vibrations, movements, blur and afterimages. My artwork has evolved into presentations of various grid comparisons: different sizes, angles and colors. The use of color progressions are now used to support the effects of the changing grid patterns. Color, while still a priority, is now secondary in significance to the grid patterns. By using various grids, I intend to create an ambiguous space, a surface that one can get lost in, and the side effect is that perceptual abstractions add to the retinal experience.

David Kuntzman received his bachelor's in art and painting from The University of Mount Union and did postgraduate work at Kent State University. He has recently shown his work at the Little Art Gallery, The Butler Institute of American Art and the Massillon Museum, among others. He currently runs David L. Kuntzman Insurance Agency, and is the president and co-owner of Imaginatives, Inc., makers of Christopher Pop-In-Kins. He serves on various boards and serves many organizations.

CONTACT: davidk@popinkins.com

TED LAWSON

The watercolor medium allows me to use the basic principles and elements of design to create exciting images. My images are two-way streets. On the one hand, they are a self-expression for me, and on the other, they are a glimpse into my being. The range of subject matter around me is diverse and immense. My immediate response to the subject matter becomes a snapshot in time as I begin to explore the shapes that make up the composition. This process is more than just recording facts. It is a process that enhances the two-way street. Observing people in their everyday lives is exciting to me. Developing scenes of everyday life allows me to be a part of people's lives and the communities where they live. The resulting product is often a pleasant surprise because of the spontaneity of the medium.

Ted Lawson's initial art training came during high school in Phoenix, Ariz. He had always remained interested in art, but a tour in the US Navy and a career in engineering interrupted his early progress. Lawson has since studied with nationally-known instructors Gerald Brommer, Tony Couch and Fred Graff, and continues training and development in watercolor composition and design. Lawson works in watercolors and acrylics primarily in a representational style, however he experiments with non-objective and abstract styles. Born in Terre Haute, Ind., he resides in Canton, Ohio, with his wife Patricia, a high school Spanish teacher. He is a Signature Member of the Ohio Watercolor Society, and while he got a late start, he is an award-winning artist and has been juried into regional, state and international exhibitions.

CONTACT: www.TedLawsonArtist.com

JEFF LOWE

I have had a passion for photography for most of my life. I remember burning through roll after roll of film and never being satisfied with the result. Over the years, my hobby has transformed into something more than "just taking pictures." I have found myself becoming more and more enthralled with abstract and fine art photography. As my craft developed, I have found myself drawn to a unique angle at an exact moment, without manipulating composition.

I've had no formal education in photography, but I fell in love with it and after awhile I started to think I could do it. It has taken many years and several thousand photos before I felt comfortable calling myself a photographer. I'm still struggling with the idea of calling myself an artist, and I am both humbled and honored to be included in such an incredible and creative group.

I've developed as a photographer from learning by doing - finding out what works and what doesn't (especially what doesn't). Expressing my personal perspective, I try to capture the beautiful simplicity of what I see, a brief instant frozen in time. Through photography, I have found an outlet for my creative expression. I am able to capture and share some of what is going on inside my head.

Jeff Lowe is entirely self-taught in the ways of digital, 35mm and medium format film through years of studying images created by others, reading technical books and mostly from just plain shooting. His current focus is fine art, and he seeks the abstract, whether it be in nature or in an everyday object in the home.

CONTACT: www.JeffLoweStudios.com

BILLY LUDWIG

Impale Design: The Artwork of **Billy Ludwig** is digital artwork that focuses on the paranormal and the macabre. It is a mix of the contemporary and the surreal.

CONTACT: www.ImpaleDesign.com

JASPER
DIGITAL DESIGN, © 2010

43

JOANNE MARIOL

I photograph objects that most people wouldn't give a second glance, but somehow they always seem to stop me dead in my tracks. It may be a classic car's swooping fender, a row of carousel horses waiting for another go-round or an old motel sign with blinking neon announcing "vacancy." My photographs may look like they were taken long ago in another place, but that image of the Tilt-A-Whirl isn't from 1950's Coney Island. It's the ride you threw up on last summer at the Stark County Fair. That motel sign is the one that you pass by every week on Lincoln Way. It looks familiar, but you're not sure where you have seen it before. These objects may be a little old and a little weathered, but they are a part of our past and my goal is for you to take a second glance at them in the present.

Joanne Mariol of Massillon, Ohio, has been shooting images of classic cars, carousels and the county fair for the past 15 years. To her, these nostalgic subjects are an art form - from the swooping fenders of a classic car to the hand painted horses on a vintage carousel - she captures and preserves these beautiful subjects in her photographs.

CONTACT: www.JoanneMariol.Blogspot.com

CAROUSEL
PHOTOGRAPHY, © 2010

44

BRETT MARRINER

I am focused on telling stories visually in as dynamic a way as possible. This piece of my work is based on the theory of the "uncanny valley," which says that when robots and other facsimiles of humans look and act almost like actual humans, it causes a response of revulsion among human observers.

So in this case, my construction droid is left sitting outside at night, like a piece of machinery, with only the rats to accompany him.

Brett Marriner is a 1999 graduate of the Art Institute of Pittsburgh for computer animation and multimedia. He has worked in the multimedia field building rich internet applications (RIA), games, tradeshow kiosks and web sites for nine years. Along the way, he has had the opportunity to work on some illustrations for clients as well. Much of his illustration work begins as ink drawings, which are later digitally-altered and colored. Marriner lives in North Canton, Ohio, with his wife and two great children.

CONTACT: www.BrettMarriner.com

UNCANNY VALLEY
INK & DIGITAL, 20" x 20", © 2010

MEGAN MARS

At first glance, a person may interpret my work as overtly sexy. To me though, my art is a way to express the female empowerment, freedom and confidence that we all seem to wish we had. I paint the beauty that lurks inside us all, if only we care to peel back the layers and look deeper.

As women, we feel this enormous pressure from society to be the supermodel all the time, the one with the perfect looks who is totally in control of everything in her life. Beneath the surface, in the depth of our hearts and souls are all of our fears and insecurities, our strengths and weaknesses. I've seen both darkness and light in every person I meet.

I always try to portray when I can women who are fearless and totally at home in their own skin, women who are intelligent and brave, who care not a bit for the criticisms of the world. You could say that the women I paint are the brave face I show to the world in place of my own. They represent to me the ongoing search for the confident Goddess inside myself.

Megan Mars was born and raised in the Canton area, spending her entire life pursuing a love affair with creativity. She has been an artist in one capacity or another since childhood, always filling free moments with creative projects and filling book after book with sketches. Creating art is her biggest passion in life, the driving force that keeps her going every day. For Mars, painting is like meditation... every brushstroke is soothing to her ever-scattered mind, and helps her stay sane in the everyday grind and mundane.

CONTACT: www.MeganMars.carbonmade.com

**INSPIRATION IS
IN THE BLOOD**
ACRYLIC, 24" x 36", © 2008

TIFFANY MARSH

I am most often inspired by the textures, colors and rhythms found in nature. For me, even in the subtlest ways, God's color combinations are always perfect. Most of my work is heavily textured and impressionistic, with loose figural elements that can excite a narrative in the viewer's imagination. I love it when people look at my work and immediately begin to form a story in their minds as to what is happening, imagining what just took place or what the subjects are thinking at the moment they are depicted. I love the challenge of expressing movement and activity in my work, and find that even in the quieter pieces, there is a kinetic sensibility - be it a feather falling, people engaged in an activity or simply the rhythm of the elements of each individual work.

Tiffany Marsh owns Bliss Studio & Gallery in downtown Canton, where she showcases local artists, gives lessons and produces her own work. She also teaches at Canton Montessori School, where she revived a near-defunct art program by bringing in local volunteer artistic talent and using inexpensive materials in unexpected ways. Before returning to her hometown of Canton, she worked in New York, designing for DKNY, The Gap and Polo Ralph Lauren. Marsh has been featured in the Museum of Art and Design in New York City. She is the 2010 winner of Hearts with Hope public art contest for the Domestic Violence Project, and is a 2010 recipient of ystark!'s Twenty Under 40! awards. She is on the board of trustees for the Canton Museum of Art and a founding member of the Canton Montessori PTO. Marsh received her bachelor's degree from Ohio Wesleyan University and studied at The Masters School in Dobbs Ferry, N.Y.

CONTACT: t4tiff@gmail.com

JUVENILE BLUEBIRD
ACRYLIC, OIL & PLASTER, 30" x 30", © 2008

JUNGLE MOON
MIXED MEDIA, 29" x 34", © 2009

JOE MARTINO

My paintings are characterized by a sense of mystery that invites the viewer in, and often there is a hint of realism hidden in the textures, colors and shapes. The discipline of content and composition is sometimes left to chance, often coming from a place that knows both intention and the freedom of the artistic spirit and may involve little structured direction. From a spontaneous beginning, to the addition of layers of color and texture, my paintings evolve toward excitement and depth and emotion.

As a former teacher of chemistry, anatomy and marine biology, I am greatly influenced by science and nature. For me, there is a strong connection between science, artistic expression and creativity. An artist friend of mine described my paintings and my palette as "organic".... I like that.

Joe Martino has been involved in the art community for most of his adult life. While his undergraduate degree was pre-med, he has been a lifelong student of the arts. He has been accepted to many juried shows, exhibited at many arts events in Northeast Ohio and has been the featured artist at the Canton Museum of Art, the Massillon Museum of Art, Kent State University and Stark State College, to name a few.

CONTACT: www.JoeMartinoArt.com

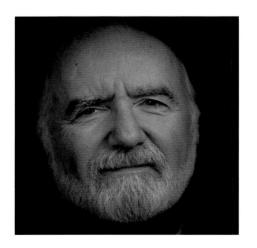

FLORALBUNDA
WATERCOLOR, 24" x 18" © 2008

NANCY STEWART MATIN

I work in watermedia in a semi-abstract manner, always pursuing new approaches. My goal is to make the spectator engage, to travel the piece and feel some of the emotion I felt in creation. I want to make you think. I want to make your day.

Nancy Stewart Matin is a watercolor artist and instructor. She is a Signature Member of the Ohio Watercolor Society. Her work is in the permanent collection at the Canton Museum of Art, the Massillon Museum of Art, Stark County District Library, North Canton Library and numerous private collections. Her work was also featured on the cover of the Canton Bicentennial Calendar.

CONTACT: alfacat@neo.rr.com

BIG SUR MARINE LAYER
WATERCOLOR, 22" x 14", © 2010

BOB MAURER

Some of the subjects that attract me include fog, forests and the rugged coasts of California and Maine. A successful painting will convey a feeling of relaxation and contemplation through the use of a delicately balanced, minimalist composition using subdued colors and subtle tonal qualities. I like to put the "water" in watercolors using wet into wet washes, letting the natural flow and blending of the medium guide me through the painting process.

Bob Maurer has specialized in watercolors and pen and ink drawings since 1972. He has studied under several artists, including Carol Barnes, Glenn Bradshaw, Bette Elliott, Fred Graff, Polly Hammet, Serge Hollerbach, Marc Moon and Hal Scroggy. He is a Signature Member of the American Society of Architectural Illustrators, Roycroft Master Artisans, Ohio Watercolor Society and Whiskey Painters of America. His work is shown at The Watercolor Gallery, Laguna Beach, Calif., Camden Falls Gallery, Camden, Maine, and The Copper Shop Gallery, East Aurora, N.Y.

CONTACT: www.BobMaurer.com

ORCHARD FRESH
COLORED PENCIL, 20" x 16", © 2005

SHARON FRANK MAZGAJ

I am continuously working in several mediums. Most of my work consists of still life examples. An avid collector of antiques, dolls, figurines and pottery, many of my works incorporate a piece from my collection. I usually include a "face" in my work. The inclusion could be an animal, insect, doll or pottery figurine. I feel this gives my work a sense of whimsy, making the viewer smile.

Sharon Frank Mazgaj exhibits her artwork in local and international juried art exhibits. She has received numerous awards and accolades for her talent. Her work was the subject of an article entitled "Personalized Still Lifes" in the September 2005 edition of American Artist Magazine. She has illustrated two books: "Carved in Stone," by Craig Peters, and "Green, Our Heritage, Our Home," by Judith P. Christy. She has donated her time and talent to painting backdrops and sets for Green's Theatre 8:15. She is a member and instructor for the Green Arts Council. A former art teacher in the Akron Public Schools, Mazgaj is a graduate of Sandy Valley High School and The University of Akron. She is a Signature Member of the Colored Pencil Society of America (CPSA) and has received awards in their annual international shows and Explore This! exhibitions. Her work has been featured at local exhibits such as the Massillon Art Show and North Canton May Show.

CONTACT: www.acorn.net/cpsadc101/mazgaj.htm

DAVID McDOWELL

"Heritage implies that its loss would be a sacrifice, and that its preservation likewise involves sacrifices." --Andre Chastel, French Art Historian

Each object that I break or cut - each bottle, each sliver or piece of glass - has its own story, its own heritage. It is my hope to capture the fast moving mind and cause it to slow down, first by capturing it with spectacle, and then drawing it in by activating the stories of the world. I am constantly bursting with stories I want to tell. I want to share them with others. I want to share the stories of these objects, comprised of many pieces made into one. I want to share the stories of the human heart, and make them into one. Most people see junk. I see beauty. Do you realize that you are not junk? You are celebrated in my art, even if even I don't know it.

David McDowell graduated in 2002 from Indiana Wesleyan University with a bachelor's in ceramics with special emphasis in sculpture and stained glass. He served as Artist in Residence for Sandy Valley High School (through an ArtsinStark initiative) where he completed the Heritage Tree. He has created work for private collectors across the country.

CONTACT: www.BurntMarshwiggleArt.com

HERITAGE TREE
ALUMINUM, LEADED GLASS &
RECLAIMED BRICK, 12' x 15' x 12', © 2010

STEPHEN McNULTY

I was raised with a deep fondness and ardor for all things wild. Sitting at home in suburbia, I often dreamt of trekking through the Amazon and finding rare or possibly undiscovered fauna. My childhood dreams were realized when I was brought on by a World Bank Special Project in Tarapoto, Peru, to track down the vanishing poison frogs of the rainforest. This was just one of many amazing sojourns for me in my experience as a conservation photographer.

Stephen McNulty has never studied photography in any formal capacity. His academic career has always focused solely on conservation dynamics and biological issues. In 2002, his studies began taking him abroad to remarkable and remote regions. By virtue of traveling to these clandestine reaches, he was afforded time with renowned photographers and cinematographers from National Geographic, the BBC and Smithsonian. These lensmen taught him what a powerful tool photography can be in the conservationist's arsenal. He uses the imagery he captures to create awareness. Speaking at schools, showing his work in galleries and shows, and lecturing for local groups, he is able to illustrate the evanescent beauty that still exists in the world and show that true wilderness is something worth protecting.

CONTACT: www.McNultyImaging.com

TIDEPOOL #12
PHOTOGRAPHY, © 2007

THOM METZ

My focus is on capturing an intriguing moment in time — that's what memories are made of!

I strive to create a mood, illustrated by light and shadow, that makes you step back in time or take another look at a familiar subject. I tend to shoot in infrared and render in semi-monotones reminiscent of B&W photography.

Thom Metz is originally from the Canton South area. He was a professional photographer and lab technician at 16, and it was his passion until his early twenties, when a career change consumed him and other priorities took over while his Hasselblad gathered dust. After managing the implementation of communication systems in 10 states and living in five regions for several years, Metz returned to Ohio. While teaching, he delved into the digital world to show students the fundamentals for web-based applications and, in turn, he has returned to the creative world of photography.

CONTACT: tmetz@neo.rr.com

WELDER
PHOTOGRAPHY, © 2009

54

LIBERTY
WATERCOLOR,
21" x 13", © 1999

WANDA MONTGOMERY

Light is a very important part of my watercolor paintings. Light is to painting as rhythm is to music ... it sets the tempo and establishes the mood. Allowing the light to dance through the composition creates a rhythmic passageway for the viewer. My intent is to capture the given mood and mystery of the moment. Using light as a means of expression allows me to accomplish this and yet leaves much to the viewer's imagination. After working in watercolor for years, I now work in mixed media (nonobjective painting) and find it very exciting. Instead of recreating what I see, I create a painting from a deeper place, letting the painting tell me what it needs. Through time, my painting experience has transpired into an incredible, never ending journey!

Wanda Montgomery has studied with numerous national and international teachers for 12 years. She ran her own art gallery in Canton, Ohio, from 2007 to 2009. Her work is in numerous public and private collections around the world. She has exhibited in shows of the Ohio Watercolor Society and the American Watercolor Society and others around the country. She has won various awards, most recently First Place, Watercolor, in the 2010 annual May Show of the Little Art Gallery in North Canton, Ohio.

CONTACT: studiowm@neo.rr.com

FIRE-BREATHING RABBITS
OIL, 14" x 11", © 2005

ERIN T. MULLIGAN

I hope that my paintings convey mixed feelings and contradictory subjects that are made to get along together within a single plane. I feel like this is the stuff that our human existence is made of, nothing is totally isolated and perceived alone by itself, I think.

Sometimes my art says something, sometimes it doesn't. Usually, my pieces tell a story, or they try to develop a particular idea, but sometimes they are just made up of things that I find funny together. I hope to make my living at being an artist, but without becoming motivated by the money aspect of what I do. I worry that if that were to happen, my art would lose its very soul.

Erin T. Mulligan is an artist who lives and works in Canton, Ohio. She has wanted to make art all the time since she was a child, especially with her grandmother and mother both being accomplished artists. When she was 15, her grandmother gave her a three-day course on how to use oil paint, teaching her the impressionist style. She began taking lessons from Frank Dale in 2003 in glazing, the technique of old Dutch painters. She continues that style in her work to this day.

CONTACT: www.ErinMulliganArt.com

SU NIMON

My art is an expression and an exploration. My background in design is evident in images that are simple and clean, while still evoking an emotional response. This basic theme runs through my digital work, acrylic and mixed medium paintings and my textile art.

Su Nimon is originally from Alliance, Ohio, but lived for many years in the greater Denver, Colo. area. She returned to Stark County in 2001 and opened Journey Studios in the downtown Canton Arts District in 2007. Her work at Journey Studios changes and evolves, but she focuses primarily upon artwork, bodywork and total wellness. Journey Studios brings to life her dream of working in only those areas that she truly loves. She believes that Journey Studios is proof positive that it is possible to make a living while living your dreams.

CONTACT: www.JourneyStudios.com

SCOT PHILLIPS

I find beauty in ephemeral things and in tiny details. I work with themes of disintegration, loss and obsession. I speak of impermanent things, which will eventually come to an end. These things can range from possessions to relationships. In my work, I use materials such as drain cleaners, oils, earth and stains, etc., creating bases that in time will rot. With the completion of a piece, it takes on an appearance that I know with time will change. I sometimes use screened pictures, creating a contrast between an eternal image and a canvas that cannot hold that image permanently.

Scot Phillips was born and has lived in Massillon his whole life. He is a recent graduate of Kent State University, with a bachelor's degree in art history/fine arts. Currently, he is the membership coordinator at the Massillon Museum. Phillips held his first solo exhibition in conjunction with the Ananda Center's "Art Displaced: Neighborhood Natives" series in 2008. He plans to pursue a master's degree in art history, focusing on the criticism of modern art.

CONTACT: www.TheBlakHorse.com

CINÉ
ACRYLIC, 22" x 32", © 2010

TINA PUCKETT

I enjoy seeing things in the world that many others miss. I find that behind the lens of a camera, there is a bit of Zen existence where nothing exists but me and the focus, and that moment of trying to frame the "perfect" shot. I am moved by great poetry and can be brought to tears by dance. I think the best creativity comes from tempering emotion into art and seeing things in a different perspective than the world sometimes gives us time to see.

Tina Puckett is a Stark County resident who works in poetry and photography. She served as editor-in-chief for the literary magazine, *Canto*, from 1995 to 1998. She is currently pursuing an MFA in creative writing and enjoys nearly all forms of art as a participant or spectator.

CONTACT: www.TinaPuckett.webs.com

ASWIRL
PHOTOGRAPHY, © 2009

MIEZE RIEDEL

As I grew up, my parents instilled in me a love for the natural splendor of the world. When I see a lovely creation of nature or an interesting setting, I think: "Oh, I have to paint this!"

Painting gives me pleasure and an opportunity to share my impressions with others as realistic views or as abstractions. Materials, tools and colors used in painting are a challenge to my imagination. Therefore, I experiment with the possibilities offered by different papers, colors and styles. There is so much to explore and I hope I will never be restricted by settling on one style or genre. I feel this would stunt my further development in the skills required for the art of painting.

Mieze Riedel loved to paint and draw from childhood on. She studied architecture, and later pursued a career in watercolor painting. She studied with many nationally-known painters in classes and workshops, and taught for eight years at the Alliance, Ohio, Art Center. Her work is in collections worldwide, and she is a member of many art organizations. She is a Signature Life Member of the Transparent Watercolor Society of America, and the Ohio and Georgia Watercolor Societies. Her work has won numerous awards while appearing in over 30 national and regional exhibitions.

CONTACT: mhriedel@earthlink.net

PAT RIPPLE

I endeavor to capture the mood or essence of a place, object or person. I enjoy working "in the field" and most of my work is the result of sketches done on location. Watercolor is my first choice and continues to be a favorite medium of mine, but my experience with various mediums keeps my enthusiasm at its peak!

Pat Ripple is well known locally for her watercolor landscapes, seascapes and still life paintings. She has taught classes at the Massillon Museum, in her home and at other locations throughout the years. A native Ohioan, she was born and raised in Massillon. While attending The University of Akron School of Art for three years, she was introduced to both oil and acrylic mediums as well as watercolor. In workshops across the country, with many nationally recognized teachers of the arts, her style has evolved. Ripple has exhibited her works in regional and national shows and has received numerous awards. Her work can be found in many private and corporate collections. She is a Signature Member of the Ohio Watercolor Society, Whiskey Painters of America, The Massillon Museum, Canton Museum of Art Artists League and The Massillon Community Artists.

CONTACT: mripple@sbcglobal.net

ABANDONED
WATERCOLOR, 19.5" x 26.5", © 1998

PRISCILLA ROGGENKAMP

Time and physical space, location and experience, layers and materials, memory and memorial all influence my work. The references in my work are the result of responding to experience and place rather than simply documenting it. I have an interest in abstract visual expression and the dialogue between the artwork, the artist and the viewer.

Priscilla Roggenkamp was born in Bangor, Maine, and has resided with her family in Alliance since 1990, teaching and making art. She studied art at Kent State University (MFA), University of Arkansas (M.Ed.) and Heidelberg College (BA). Working primarily in drawing and painting, she began creating three-dimensional work in the mid '90s. In 2003, she and Keith McMahon began sharing studio space, leading them to create collaborative sculptures. She has taught at The College of Wooster, the University of Mount Union, Canton Country Day School, Blue Ridge Community College, James Madison University and the University of Arkansas. She is currently teaching at Ashland University. She has conducted workshops in Florida, Ohio and Maine and has co-authored several publications.

CONTACT: www.Studio-TwoFourteen.com

BODY
FROM "BODY, MIND AND SPIRIT"
SANDSTONE & CAST BRONZE, 12" x 18" x 8", © 2009
PHOTOGRAPH PROVIDED BY THE ARTIST

WILLIAM SHEARROW

As far back as I can remember, an artist is all I have ever wanted to be. It is my life and my passion. Clay is the most interesting medium to express my vision. I love the unpredictable nature of ceramics. Taking a material as unpredictable as clay and transforming it with hand and fire into a work of art never fails to thrill me. I believe every pot holds its own unique personality, yet still reflects the artist who first gave it life.

William Shearrow was born and raised in Canton, Ohio. He has made a living as a ceramic artist since graduating with a BFA in ceramics from Columbus College of Art & Design. He has his own studio and has been teaching ceramics at the Canton Museum of Art for more than 20 years.

CONTACT: www.ShearrowPottery.com

HORSE HAIR RAKU
PORCELAIN, 15" x 5", ©2010

SARAH WINTHER SHUMAKER

I love to experiment with every medium I can get my hands on. I don't set out to produce artwork that makes a statement about one thing or another anymore. For me, the joy is in creating pieces that play with color, shapes, texture and the materials involved - both traditional and non-traditional. Combining elements that don't ordinarily "go together" is one of my favorite challenges. Much of life involves looking - really looking at things - and discovering the many layers or details involved. I enjoy creating artwork wherein the observer discovers something new, uncovers a new layer or notices a new detail with each viewing.

Sarah Winther Shumaker is a mixed-media artist from North Canton, Ohio, who is always ready and willing to experiment with her art supplies. Shumaker has been an artist all of her life (just ask her parents), and began exhibiting her work in 2005. She has won three First Place awards in the North Canton May Show and an Honorable Mention in the Stark County Artist Exhibition at the Massillon Museum. Her work has been in other Stark County juried and invitational shows - including Sensory Feast, Blind Date, Fibernation and 28 Variations. Shumaker has a master's degree in education and works as an outreach coordinator for ArtsinStark. She teaches art classes for children through adults - including in-service workshops for teachers.

CONTACT: www.SarahShumaker.com

WALLFLOWER
STONEWARE, 10" x 10" x 8", © 2007

HURSHEL SMITH

My objective in my work is to show the beauty nature has to offer, in a different and unique art form. Using only the finest, top quality exotic and domestic woods, I design my creations basically by thought. Fortunately, I am one of those people who can pick up a piece of wood and see the finished creation in my mind.

Each of my works is assembled piece-by-piece and turned on a wood lathe to create the unique shape and size. The average vessel is in my shop for approximately two months; but some pieces have taken much longer. My wife is invaluable to my work and my process.

Hurshel Smith started working with wood in high school wood shop and is largely self-taught. In 1997, he started creating pieces as gifts for family and friends and later contacted Lazar's Creative Framing & Art Gallery in Canton about putting his work on consignment. With success in the gallery, he later ventured into the juried fine art and fine craft shows, and has since received many awards. He retired from The Timken Company in 1998 after 31 years of employment.

CONTACT: www.WoodCreationsbyHursh.com

THE KING'S CUP
WOOD, 9" x 13" OVERALL
© 2006

THE THOUGHTFUL WINEMAKER
OIL, 18" x 22", © 2008

BRITTANY STEIGERT

My works are spaces of nostalgia. Familiar subjects nestled within ambiguous alcoves create visual comfort, while layers of process, involving addition and subtraction of material, lend aesthetic complexity as well as literal and figurative depth. My oil paintings on canvas and assemblages, created with fabric, bleach, paint and oftentimes wax, are all reminiscent of each other. They reveal and conceal the evidence of processes that allow the artwork to unfold as it is created, often with quite unexpected results! Born out of grief, my earlier works are mostly melancholy. Wistfulness and contemplation have brought a particular earnestness to my recent work.

Brittany Steigert is a Malone University graduate with a bachelor's degree in fine art. From her senior display in high school to her more recent college exhibition, she has developed skills not only in creating art, but in introducing it to a wider audience. Steigert has shown her works on campus and in downtown Canton. Her career has included not only displaying art for the community in galleries, but involving the community by sharing what she has learned, specifically in the ceramics arena, as a teacher for adult and children's ceramics at the Massillon Museum.

CONTACT: www.BLSteigert.com

JUDITH STERLING

My art has forever been my saving grace. It has been the part of my life that helps me believe in myself, a way to be in touch with my soul, my centering. Sculpture, and the infinite variety of materials available for its creation, fascinates me. Each material has a life of its own, like a living person. Mastering my art is the love of stroking the material to find its inherent strength and then pushing it to its limits in form and grace, while understanding the weakness of the material and knowing it must be respected in order to push the sculpture to a strong and beautiful life of its own. In art, as in life, we mold and fashion our existence from all that is before us and in us.

Judith Sterling knew that she had an artist's soul from a very young age, but circumstance kept her from that dream. When her children went off to school, Sterling, too, went to work studying with various masters. In 2005, with her BFA in hand, she sold her house and car, put her belongings in storage and moved to Florence, Italy, to study classical methods of high relief clay and marble sculpting at the Lorenzo De'Medici School of Art, where she found the true meaning of sculpture and the essence of form. She returned to Canton, Ohio, to pursue her career in stone and clay.

CONTACT: www.JudithSterling.com

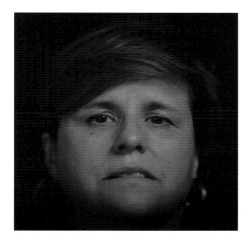

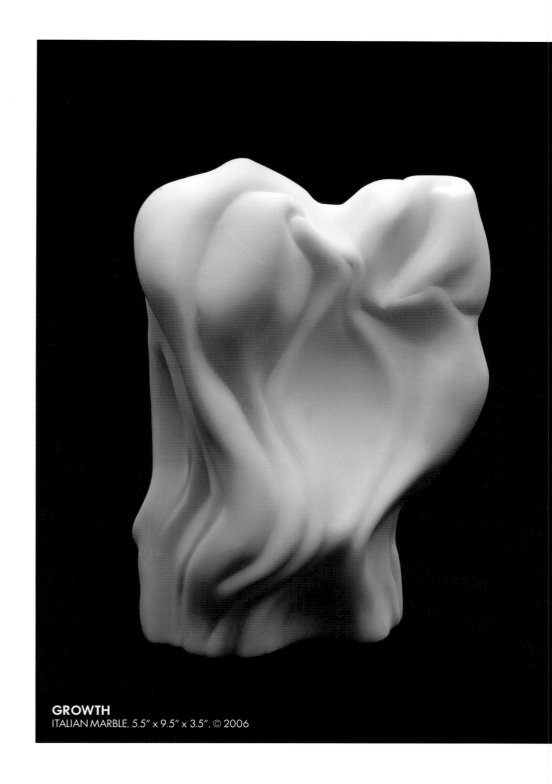

GROWTH
ITALIAN MARBLE, 5.5" x 9.5" x 3.5", © 2006

JOHN STRAUSS

When I am working on designs, different threads of my life, background and training are at play in my mind. While in the creative design mode, these threads become woven into my process: hiding and playing in my father's Chicago furniture showroom as a young boy; learning about art and architectural history and having first-hand access to Frank Lloyd Wright and Louis Sullivan buildings in Chicago; or building Art Deco reproductions, gaining a love for subtle curves, exotic veneers and classical proportions that displaced embellished decoration. I take this baggage into my wood shop, unpack it, and try to make things for people that enhance their personal space, that lend dignity to their lives, and that add a piece of handcrafted creativity to their homes.

John Strauss has 20 years of experience creating and manufacturing furniture for designers and architects. He has worked with top designers from around the country to fabricate custom designs, has created works for sacred spaces and has launched a line of his own designs. He takes his inspiration from the Art Deco masters. Born in Chicago, Strauss grew up in the "furniture world." His great-aunt was Mabel Schamberg, the interior designer of the "House of Tomorrow" at the 1933 Chicago Worlds' Fair. His father owned a high-end furniture showroom in downtown Chicago, and his mother is an interior designer. Strauss trained as a sculptor with an undergraduate degree from Brown University and a master's of fine arts degree from City University of New York. He moved to New York City for a fellowship with the Whitney Museum Independent Study Program, where he was introduced to his current craft.

CONTACT: www.StraussFurniture.com

GABLE ENTRY TABLE
WALNUT, EUROPEAN ZEBRAWOOD & HAND-
FORGED IRON WORK, 46" x 34.5" x 16" , © 2008
PHOTOGRAPH PROVIDED BY THE ARTIST

AUTUMNAL SUNRISE
WATER-BASED OILS, 40" x 30", © 2005

CHRISTOPHER J. TRINER

Color is a powerful emotion and causes many different reactions in people. I feel color can tell a story with little in the way of defined images. Sometimes the mystery is half the fun!

Christopher J. Triner is a Stark County native and has been a professional artist for the past 25 years. Triner teaches visual art at Hoover High School in the North Canton City School District.

CONTACT: ctriner1@neo.rr.com

ANGELINA VERGINIS

As an art teacher for grades K-8 for the last 14 years and an amateur photographer since my teen years, I have always loved to look for the beauty that surrounds us and share it with others. Whether it's in the details of simple things, or stolen moments preserved in an image, documenting beauty in visible forms is an inspiring celebration of life.

Angelina Verginis has taught art at Southeast Local Schools and serves as an art instructor for the Massillon Museum. She received her bachelor's degree in visual arts from the College of Wooster and her master's in teaching from Marygrove College. She has participated in shows at Studio M at the Massillon Museum and 2nd April Galerie in downtown Canton. She currently displays work at the office of Dr. Patibandla in Canton, Ohio, and at Stephanie's Garden of Eden in Massillon, Ohio.

CONTACT: verginisart@yahoo.com

FREDLEE VOTAW

As I travel the long artist's road, I constantly reflect on the vision and the health of my "artist's footprint." I describe my works as contemporary "Diary Art," responses to life, the world and my emotions. Instead of writing these responses down, as one would do in a diary, I choose to release them visually, in oils or multimedia creations. My works are not pristine and slick, they are worn and faded, scratched and dented, eroded and weathered...patched over by the layers of memories, thoughts and cares that grow within an artist. I grew up in a family of folk artists: quilters, carvers, weavers...farm folk. Through them, I learned to love the faded cloth, the rusty iron, the tarnished copper and the patina on old wood. They also immersed me in all the things that are family and convinced me that the only thing that will bring you true happiness is people, not things. They instilled in me a constant desire to investigate the chambers of the heart, where only the most mysterious aspects of love reside. These are all a part of my work and the force behind my "artist's footprint."

Fredlee Votaw has exhibited works of art in solo, group and competitive shows for over 45 years, winning numerous awards on the state and national level. His works are in private, corporate and public collections across America. He has judged numerous state and national art shows and has been the keynote speaker at state, national and international visual art/computer art conferences including: Oxford, Cambridge and London, England. He has studied at The Arts Academy at the University of San Francisco, Calf., Pratt Art Institute, Brooklyn, N.Y., The Art Institute of Pittsburgh, Pittsburgh, Pa., Kent State University, The University of Akron and Ashland Universities. He has taught at the University of San Francisco, Kent State University, The University of Akron and Canton Museum of Art, and Canton McKinley, East Canton and West Branch High Schools. His honors include being named 1981 Ohio Teacher of the Year, Jennings Scholar, Fulbright-Hays Study Abroad Finalist (Netherlands), International CARN Conference Presenter (England), Featured Artist-American Artist Magazine, Kent State University Ph.D. Study Abroad Program (France and Spain) and Toyota Teacher Study Abroad Finalist (Japan).

CONTACT: www.FredleeVotaw.com

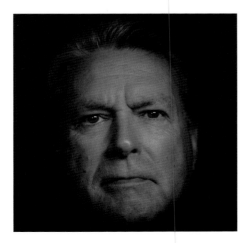

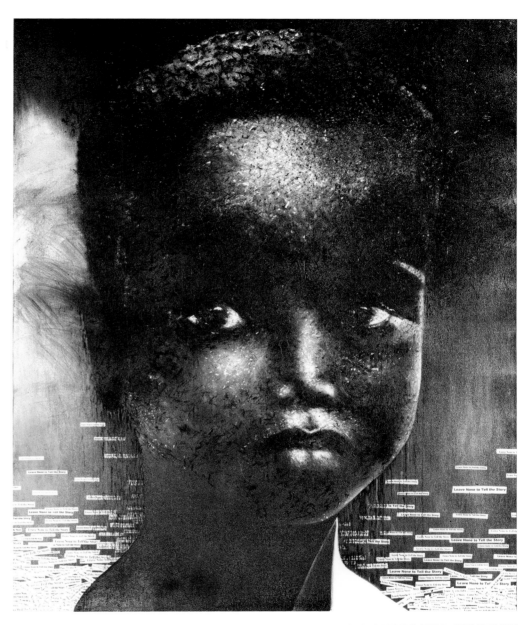

LEAVE NONE TO TELL THE STORY
OIL, 29" x 36" © 2009

MICHELE WAALKES

Art has become a meaningful way for me to process and explore the complexities of life in tandem with living it. I am committed to creating and exhibiting my artwork, which has been exhibited in various regional and national venues. My current work utilizes a variety of different methods to transfer my photography onto fabric and other surfaces. I often integrate layers to create juxtapositions, conveying visual and conceptual depth. Recurring themes in my work include the transience of life in time, as well as the feelings evoked by diverse natural, cultural, and architectural spaces.

Michele Waalkes was born in Michigan and earned her bachelor's in art from Malone University, with emphases in fibers and graphics. She currently resides in Canton, Ohio, with her husband and three children. In addition to creating her own artwork, Waalkes is also a freelance curator and is involved in many local arts programing projects. Her work utilizes her own photography, which she transfers onto various surfaces using different methods. Her work has been exhibited in various Ohio venues including The Little Art Gallery in North Canton, Kent State University at Stark Campus Gallery 6000, the Massillon Museum, 2nd April Galerie, Malone University and Anderson Creative in Canton. She has also exhibited in national venues such as the Sixth Street Gallery, Vancouver, Wash.; The Washington Gallery of Photography, Bethesda, Md.; and in the Chicago Arts District Exhibition Space, Chicago, Ill.

CONTACT: www.MicheleWaalkes.blogspot.com

PARALLEL
MIXED MEDIA, 17" x 21", © 2008

MICHAEL WEISS

I believe in telling stories through art. It is my job as an illustrator to capture in images what an author puts into words; not to compete, but to complement a story. And like a writer's vocabulary, an artist has a visual vocabulary that is reflected in the clues that enhance the viewer's experience.

Michael Weiss is the associate graphics editor at *The Repository*, Stark County's award-winning newspaper. He has been a staff artist and designer with the paper since 1996. He received his BFA from The University of Akron with a major in fine art and a minor in illustration.

CONTACT: MichaelWeiss.carbonmade.com

KEITH WILSON

In my architectural illustrations I strive to depict light, space, materials, activity and use of the facility with the intended audience in mind.

Keith Wilson is the architectural illustrator/designer of Architecture Illustrated, a leading digital architectural rendering, concept design and animation firm for architects and developers. Having worked in the industry since 1977, Wilson has been involved in projects for international clientele, including: EA Sports, Diebold, Automotive Events, YMCA and Mercedes-Benz. Raised in Canton, Ohio, he now lives with his wife, Vicki, and two sons, Keith and David. He has written articles for Modelvision Newsletter and has been featured in Diebold's newsletter. He frequently has his renderings printed in *The Repository* newspaper to give the Stark County community a visual of future architectural projects that are being developed. Wilson also plays the drums in various musical groups and for his church.

CONTACT: www.ArchitectureIllustrated.biz

SHAWN WOOD

Let me quote Lewis Hine, "If I could say it in words, I wouldn't need to photograph."

I went to Fort Apache, Ariz., with this torn American flag. I was on a mission to find a Native American to drape with this flag and take this portrait. The history of "how the West was won" has always amazed me. In the end, we basically destroyed their culture, took their land and introduced them to alcohol.

This is Ralph. He is full-blooded Apache. I found Ralph walking on Route 73, three miles outside of Fort Apache. I call this "Broken Promises."

Shawn Wood opened his commercial photography studio in 1985. The Canton Advertising Club soon awarded him the Outstanding New Member award in 1986. Though the years, he has received many awards for his outstanding photography. In 2006, he was elected president of the Cleveland Chapter of The American Society of Media Photographers. Whether photographing the integrity of the protective heat tiles on the Space Shuttle Atlantis, or a one-on-one portrait session with First Lady Barbara Bush, he has always added his own creative style. He's been featured in publications like *National Geographic* and *People Magazine*. When not shooting for assignment, his passion is creating fine art of the world he sees through the camera's lens.

CONTACT: www.Studio7Photography.com

BROKEN PROMISES
PHOTOGRAPHY, © 1997

ISABEL ZALDIVAR

Observing nature is what inspires my work in abstract and impressionistic ways. My paintings can take many directions. This gives me the freedom to make decisions in designing and composition. By constantly evaluating and applying layers of color, I try to coordinate imagination with reality. I enjoy the process of my work. I am always exploring, experimenting with different avenues without eliminating recognizable imagery.

Isabel Zaldivar has lived in Canton, Ohio, for 37 years. She graduated from the University of Cordoba, Argentina. She has studied art at Kent State University at Stark, took art, drawing and visual organization under Robert Wagner, and has studied design with Bette Elliot's class, a group of related artists, for 30 years. She continues her studies with well known artists like Ed Whitney, Carol Barner and others. She has been accepted into many juried shows and honored with many awards. Zaldivar is a Signature Member of the Ohio Watercolor Society.

CONTACT: IsabelArtStudio@sssnet.com

DEREK ZIMMERMAN

You've been bought. And a 29-year-old rat-in-a-cage turned artist, Derek Zimmerman, is paying for your way back.

But money won't buy your way out of the mirk and mire - my art will.

Fueled by a drive to give people the wake-up call that freedom of choice is an illusion, my graphic designs force you to ponder the workings of Big Brother, the inevitable revolt of nature against humanity, and the hype you've bought since Public Enemy asked you not to believe it. Images ranging from paintings, drawings, silkscreens and digital imaging force you to reconcile the art I create and its meaning in relation to the "real" world that has been constructed for you.

Derek Zimmerman is passionate about screen printing, digital imaging, painting, drawing and, of course, thinking for himself.

CONTACT: www.dwrex.com

INDEX

ACKNOWLEDGEMENTS

In producing our first book, Indigo Ink Press owes an immeasurable debt to many individuals and organizations. I only wish there were more pages with which we could elaborate on your generosity:

First and foremost, to the **69 artists immortalized in this slim yet potent volume** - thank you for sharing your creativity and eccentric passion with our press, and in turn, with every reader of this book. I think it's clear that when I say we couldn't have done this without you, you know I mean it. Quite literally.

Thanks also to all of the other artists who are working so hard in our community to bring an arts renaissance, infusing culture into the landscape of our little neck of the woods. More than 160 artists submitted work for consideration, and while we were sorry to have to disappoint some of you, we appreciate you more than you know.

A sincerest of thanks to the **Board of Trustees of Indigo Ink**, for always saying yes, for believing in the idea of a nonprofit press in Canton, for turning that idea into an actuality, and for being convinced of the success of this, our first project together. Thank you now and always to **David Kaminski**, president, **Elizabeth Jacob**, treasurer, **Tim Belden**, **Sue Grabowski** and **Cindy Staudt**, our inaugural board.

To the **Advisory Committee** - for taking on the arduous and time-consuming task of selecting these 69 exceptional artists and choosing the perfect piece to represent each of their eclectic talents. Our gratitude to the generosity of **Al Albacete**, *Canton Museum of Art*, **Robb Hankins**, *ArtsinStark*, **Gail Martino**, *Stark County Educational Service Center*, **Margo Miller**, *The University of Mount Union*, **Christine Shearer**, *Fowler Artistic Resources* and **Todd Walburn**, *2nd April Galerie*.

To three of the most talented and devoted lensmen that I've ever had the fortune to work with: **Michael Barath**, *Just Us Two Photography*, **Tim Belden**, *The Joseph Saxton Gallery of Photography* and **Thom Metz**, *independent photographer*. These lensmen photographed (beautifully!) the artwork of *Stark ARThology* and created the artist portraits in this book. Photographing and painstakingly retouching 140 photographs is certainly no small task. In these men the term perfection finds its equal.

Thanks to the **Canton Museum of Art**, **Al Albacete**, **Mary Byrne**, **Lynnda Arrasmith** and the entire staff for their collaborative spirit and hard work in making the Stark ARThology companion exhibit at the museum a reality. I can't imagine a more perfect way to celebrate the launch of this exhibit on paper than with an exhibit in one of the most illustrious arts venues in Northeast Ohio. Thank you for giving Canton's newest arts organization such a warm welcome.

Thank you to Indigo Ink's dedicated volunteer sales manager, **Doug Bennett**, for working so hard at getting our first book into stores and galleries around the county. Best salesman-slash-husband ever. And to **Marci Lynn Saling**, an exquisite event planner and a dear friend of Indigo Ink, who put together an incredible art book launch party, the coolest shindig this town has ever seen.

Last, but certainly not least - thank you to **ArtsinStark** for generously granting funds to Indigo Ink Press, an organization that, at the time, was only an idea on paper. Thank you for your faith; for seeing the possibility we only hoped to convey. As for the good work you do for Stark County's arts movement, that is a debt that none of us can ever hope to fully repay.

THE COMMITTEE

M.J. ALBACETE • Canton Museum of Art
During his 35-year tenure at The Canton Museum of Art, Albacete has juried many regional art exhibitions and has authored several articles on prominent area artists. His book, "Clyde Singer's America" (KSU Press), was nominated for an Ohioana Library Award and his two former publications on "Architecture in Canton" are still in demand. Albacete was named "Outstanding Museum Professional" by the Ohio Museums Association in 2000.

ROBB HANKINS • ArtsinStark, The County Arts Council
Hankins has spent the last 30 years directing city, county and state arts agencies in eight different states, including Wisconsin, Connecticut, California and Oregon. He has managed annual arts campaigns, arts festivals, public art projects, arts education programs and downtown arts districts. Hankins has served as president & CEO of ArtsinStark since 2005.

GAIL MARTINO • Stark Educational Service Center
Martino is an arts education consultant for the Stark County Educational Service Center. In addition to being an art lover and educator, she supports the arts in Stark County by serving on the boards of the Canton Symphony Orchestra, The Massillon Artful Living Program and IlluminArts of Stark County. Martino previously served as K-12 curriculum director in both Minerva Local Schools and Louisville City Schools.

MARGO MILLER • University of Mount Union
Miller is currently assistant professor of art and director of the Crandall Gallery at the University of Mount Union in Alliance, Ohio. She received her MFA from Kent State University and BFA from The University of Akron. She has taught at the Cleveland Institute of Art, Youngstown State University, The University of Akron and Kent State University. She has exhibited her art nationally and internationally.

CHRISTINE FOWLER SHEARER • Fowler Artistic Resources
Shearer is an independent consultant with over 12 years experience in the museum field. She provides support services for artists, collectors and nonprofit organizations. Shearer served as the executive director of the Massillon Museum from 2003 to 2010. Before coming to the Massillon Museum, she served as the first full-time executive director of the Cleveland Artists Foundation.

TODD WALBURN • 2nd April Galerie
Walburn is one of the founding members of the downtown Canton Arts District. He founded 2nd April Galerie with partner Brennis Booth in 2002, where he selects the works of local artists to showcase. Over the years, they have broadened their focus to include both visual and performing arts, with the addition of the Kathleen Howland Theatre. The downtown Canton location also provides space for more than a dozen artists to operate independently with 2nd April's "gallery in a gallery" format.

ABOUT ARTSINSTARK • The County Arts Council
ArtsinStark's mission is to use the arts to create smarter kids, new jobs and healthier communities. The organization was founded in 1968 to build the Cultural Center for the Arts. Today, ArtsinStark gives out grants, manages the Cultural Center and runs the Annual Arts Campaign. Its $2.6 million operating budget is generated almost entirely (99%!) from the private sector, earned or raised from individuals, companies and foundations. During the 2009 campaign, in the middle of a recession, the annual arts campaign raised the highest amount in over 40 years - $1.45 million. For more information, visit: www.ArtsinStark.com.